GREAT BRITISH
CARS

GREAT BRITISH CARS

A PICTORIAL HISTORY

MIRCO DE CET

AURA

This edition reprinted in 2019/C by Baker & Taylor (UK) Limited,
Bicester, Oxfordshire OX26 4ST

Copyright © Arcturus Holdings Limited
26/27 Bickels Yard, 151–153 Bermondsey Street
London SE1 3HA.

ISBN: 978-1-78599-888-1
AD005674UK

Printed in China

Contents

Introduction

From Daimler, Lanchester and Rolls-Royce to Rover, Aston Martin and Morris, the British Motor Industry has produced some of the most beautiful, glamorous and outstandingly engineered cars ever built, but it's fair to say it's never been plain sailing.

In the 19th century, car-makers were hindered by the introduction of tyrannical legislation, or the Red Flag Acts as they were known. While these new regulations may have been crucial in establishing a regulatory framework – they introduced key concepts such as vehicle registration, number plates, and the ground rules for highway authorities – they put the brakes on the development of the motor car, which at the time was seen very much as a passing phase, a toy for the rich!

Perhaps the most restrictive clause in the Acts required self-propelled motor vehicles to be accompanied by a crew of three at all times, with a maximum speed of 2mph in towns and cities. Fortunately, the most onerous restrictions were overturned by the Locomotives on Highways Act of 1896, which cleared the way ahead for further development.

It was the ingenuity and passion of a few men, with backing from the royal family, that finally set the British Motor Industry free. The now-famous annual London to Brighton run, which began in 1896, continues to celebrate their courage and conviction, with many vehicles of the period still covering the distance from Hyde Park in London to the Brighton seafront. Cars were built to last back then.

In the years that followed, the industry flourished. New ideas and better manufacturing techniques helped to transform models, and everybody benefitted. Remarkably, by the 1950s, the UK had become the second-largest manufacturer of cars in the world, next to the USA, and was out on its own as the single largest exporter in the year 1950.

There's never been a lack of Great British design, but the industry has not always operated at full throttle. The late 1960s and early 1970s saw car-making go into decline with the introduction of unattractive products, constant labour disputes and too many quality and supplier problems; stiffer competition from abroad didn't help either. In the 1980s we saw some famous names disappear altogether – this was a dark period for the British Motor Industry. By the 1990s several well-known British car marques had been sold to foreign companies; but it was pleasing to see their new owners investing in them, while also continuing to manufacture in the UK.

These days, the UK has a strong design and technical base, with lots of foreign companies carrying out research and development here. On the motorsport side of the industry, many of the companies who manufacture and supply racing teams, such as those in Formula One, are also based in the UK. The owners may have changed, but their allegiance to this country remains strong.

Since there have been so many great British cars, it was hard to decide which ones to include and which to leave out. Starting with 'Pioneers', the selection on these pages is the author's personal choice. We hope you enjoy it.

Pioneers

Daimler and the Start of an Industry

Frederick Richard Simms was a young and enthusiastic engineer who was determined to overcome all obstacles standing in the way of his dream to build cars. He was born in Hamburg of English parents and educated in Germany and London. In 1889, at the age of 26, he befriended Gottlieb Daimler. This was a meeting that was not only to shape his personal destiny, but that also laid the foundation stone for the creation of the British automotive industry.

Frederick Richard Simms

Master car-maker

Gottlieb Daimler, son of a master baker, was born in Schorndorf near Stuttgart on 17 March 1834. Working with his fellow countryman Wilhelm Maybach, Daimler built the very first four-wheel 'horseless carriage', the *Stahlradwagen* (steel wheel wagon), in 1889, which was powered by one of the engines they had constructed.

Daimler and Maybach put another engine to good use, fitting it to a 15-foot boat that achieved a top speed of 6 knots on the Neckar river. This was regarded as the first motor-boat and the supply of engines for boats became their main outlet for a while. Their engines also powered street cars and trolley buses, but the other successful fitment came in a hot-air balloon. Daimler successfully flew one over Seelberg, the 'Cannstatt' on 10 August 1888.

Simms & Co. Engineering Consultants was created in 1891 with a view to commercializing the Daimler patents in Britain, but Simms was up against some pretty formidable anti-automobile laws at the time. Undaunted, he and several of his close friends formed the Daimler Motor Syndicate Ltd in May 1893. They set up a workshop under Putney Bridge in London and proceeded to fit Daimler engines into river launches, demonstrating them to a wide-eyed public from Eel Pie Island on the Thames.

The Honourable Evelyn Ellis, a seasoned traveller, was also interested in the developing motor industry in France and Germany in the 1890s and, like Simms, became a pioneer in promoting motor vehicles in the UK. In June 1895, he

Top: Gottlieb Daimler
Below: Wilhelm Maybach

9

Gottlieb Daimler's workshop in the garden house of his villa in Taubenheimstrasse in Cannstatt. The world's first high-speed gasoline engine was built here in 1883.

ordered a left-hand drive motor car from the Paris firm of Panhard-Levassor powered by a Daimler engine. After crossing the Channel, it went by train to Micheldever station in Hampshire, where it was picked up by Ellis and Simms, who took it on a 55-mile test run to Datchet in Berkshire. Despite rumours, it was never actually stopped by the police, but it did arouse great interest as the first motor car to be driven long-distance in the UK.

Towards the end of the 19th century, bureaucrats drew up screeds of legislation that seemed to be designed to suffocate the UK automotive industry at birth. Perhaps unsurprisingly, much of the red tape was dreamt up by the lobbyists of the powerful railway industry. Their main concern was the possibility of competition, which might affect their shares. A further drawback came in the form of the Locomotives Acts, which not only restricted horseless vehicles to a speed of 2mph in towns and 4mph in the country, but also required a person walking at least 60 yards in front waving a red flag.

The ground-breaking four-stroke engine developed by Daimler and Maybach, nicknamed 'the Grandfather Clock'. The first unit ran successfully in 1884.

The 'steel-wheel car', 1889.

Harry John Lawson, a London bicycle designer, approached Simms with a view to buying his company and all the rights to Daimler products. After protracted negotiations, a team, led by Lawson, Ernest T. Hooley and Martin D. Rucker, bought the British Daimler engine patents, and all the assets that came with the Daimler Motor Syndicate. In 1896, Lawson formed and floated the Daimler Motor Company on the London Stock Market. The company purchased a lease for sixty-two-and-a-half years on the former premises of the Coventry Cotton Spinning and Weaving Company,

Below: F. R. Simms can be seen aboard the first Cannstatt–Daimler imported into England, 1895.

THE MOTOR MILLS, COVENTRY,

Represented in the above illustration, is

THE LARGEST AUTOCAR FACTORY IN THE WORLD.

Of the *four floors* of the building, **Three Floors**, giving a floor space of over **70,000 square feet**, are now being fitted up with the latest and most approved machinery for the manufacture of

AUTOCARS

under the

PENNINGTON, DAIMLER, AND BOLLEE SYSTEMS.

Most of the machinery is now in position, driven by two 500 h.p. engines, and at work upon the completion of several entirely new designs in autocars, upon which a staff of some

TWO HUNDRED HIGHLY-SKILLED WORKMEN

is now supplied by

THE GREAT HORSELESS CARRIAGE CO., LTD.

Head Offices: 40, Holborn Viaduct, London, E.C.   Works: Motor Mills, Coventry.

Far left: A driver gingerly steers his vehicle through a crowded street with a man waving his red flag (right) just ahead of him, 1896.

Left: The Motor Mills, Coventry.

which occupied a site of 13 acres with a newly re-built factory in the Midlands. After fitting out the four-storey works from end to end with suitable plant and machinery, they were ready to produce motor vehicles on a large scale.

The Prince of Wales, the future King Edward VII, wanted the chance to ride in an automobile, so Simms and Ellis obliged by taking him out in a belt-driven Daimler. The future king returned from the experience full of enthusiasm and agreed to become patron of Britain's first motor show.

Inset: The Prince of Wales' mechanic at the wheel of his 6hp Daimler, 1900.

15

With public opinion now bolstered by royal influence, the Red Flag Act was finally abolished on 14 November 1896. The occasion was celebrated by the syndicate who called up 58 vehicles to take part in a race from the UK capital to the sea. To this day, the so-called 'Emancipation Run' from London to Brighton is held on the first Sunday in November, but only for vehicles built up to 1905.

In 1900 HRH the Prince of Wales bought a 6hp Daimler with phaeton bodywork by Messrs Hooper of St James', a company that was later

Left: Edward VII updates his Daimler to an 18/24hp model in fitting with his status as king.

Above: The Daimler–Grafton tourer, 1897.

incorporated into Daimler. This started a century of royal patronage and, for many years, Daimler was the make to beat throughout the entire British sphere of influence.

In terms of publicity, the impact provided by the inaugural Brighton run was so great that the Daimler Motor Company felt confident enough to start production at their Coventry premises in 1897. The first cars to come out of the factory in January 1897 were fitted with Panhard engines, but shortly afterwards Daimler engines were introduced, and by the middle of the year they were producing three of their own cars a week.

Now came a series of fall-outs, with Simms quitting his post, Lawson resigning as chairman and just one year later Gottlieb Daimler also throwing in the towel, never having attended a single board meeting. In 1904 the company found itself in financial difficulties. But a new company took over the old one, together with its debts.

With reorganization, Daimler saw profits rise steadily, and all that was needed was stability. A takeover by the Birmingham Small Arms Company (BSA) seemed the best way forward, and it was completed in 1910.

The Daimler factory, 1908.

Lanchester

The three Lanchester brothers, Frederick, George and Frank, incorporated The Lanchester Engine Company Limited in December 1899 in Sparkbrook, Birmingham.

Their first car, which they started in 1895, used a single-cylinder 1,306cc engine and ran on public roads in 1896. By 1897, a second car with a twin-cylinder engine had been built.

The first production cars followed in 1900; six were made as demonstrators and they featured two-cylinder, horizontal, air-cooled, 4,033cc engines. A side-lever was used to steer the vehicles and the first cars were sold to the public the following year.

In 1902, Lanchester became the first company to fit disc brakes – although a little primitive, they did fit the description. All bodies for the cars came from outside

A 1902 Lanchester. Early cars used tiller steering, which was replaced as a standard fitting in 1911.

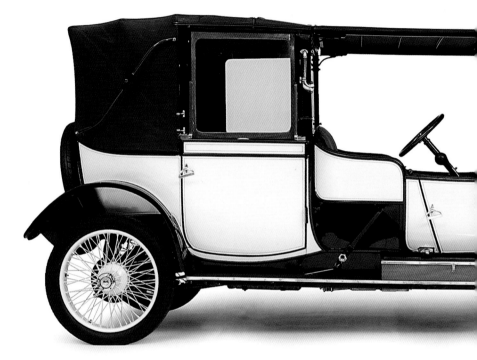

coachbuilders until 1903 when
Lanchester started building their own.

1904 saw the company put into
voluntary liquidation. It was then
recapitalized and rechristened the

Lanchester Motor Company Ltd.

1904 models featured a 2,470cc,
four-cylinder, water-cooled,
overhead-valve engine with pressure
lubrication, a novelty for the time. In

Above: The Lanchester Car Monument, Birmingham.

Above left: Blue plaque in Montgomery Street, Sparkbrook, Birmingham.

Left: A 1910 Lanchester 28hp landaulette, at the Louwman Museum in The Hague, Netherlands.

1906, a six-cylinder model joined the line-up, and by 1908 a conventional steering wheel became an option, before being made standard in 1911.

Frederick Lanchester resigned in 1913, with brother George taking over, while Frank ran the London office. The 5.5 litre, six-cylinder 'Forty' now had its engine repositioned in the conventional forward berth, but few were manufactured due to the outbreak of World War One.

23

SOLE AGENTS
SKEATES & BOCKAERT
AUCKLAND.

The Star Motor Company

The Star Motor Company started life in the bicycle world. In 1870 Edward Lisle built his own bicycle and proceeded to race it with some success. The year 1883 saw Lisle found the Star Cycle Company in Wolverhampton, producing a number of different machines. A new factory was acquired in Stewart Street in 1889, and by 1904 Star was the largest Midlands-based bicycle manufacturer.

Left: This 1898 Star was the first Star motor car in Auckland, New Zealand.

Right: Uncluttered by bodywork or other paraphernalia, this is the engine of a Star-Benz of c.1900.

The first Star car, their 1898 model, was often called the Benz-Star since it was essentially a single-cylinder 3.5hp Benz. Lisle had adopted a six-point star as the company logo in 1891 and a suit against Mercedes was successfully fought in 1902.

In 1912, Star introduced their torpedo-bodied 15.9hp model fitted with a 3,016cc, four-cylinder engine with bullnose radiator. World War One saw production cease as the company turned its attentions to war work.

Above: A 1913 12–15hp Special Streamline Star model at the Lakeland Museum, Cumbria.

Opposite: A Star No.1 racing car. The driver is Harry Godwin with his mechanic Victor George Taylor.

A 1910 15hp Star, advertised as the fastest car of its size in the country.

Herbert Austin and his partner H. H. Mulliner built this unusual Wolseley tricar in c.1896 at their Birmingham workshop when Austin was manager of the Wolseley Sheep-Shearing Machinery Company. This was Austin's first car design, and it is classed as one of the earliest British cars.

The Wolseley Autocar Number One, 1897.

Wolseley

The Wolseley Sheep Shearing Machine Company Limited was a London-incorporated company created to capitalize on a business established by Frederick Wolseley in Australia. The English part of the business, founded in 1889, was created to promote his sheep-shearing invention, specially designed to remove wool as a single fleece and thus increase its value.

Wolseley manufactured his sheep-shearing machinery largely by assembling bought-in components. Herbert Austin managed one of these suppliers and Wolseley was so impressed he employed him at his company. In November 1893, Wolseley and Austin arrived in

England to start a manufacturing operation in Broad Street, Birmingham. Wolseley resigned in 1894 because of poor health.

Austin moved the factory to new and larger premises in Aston, Birmingham and started looking at new ventures to subsidize the seasonal sheep-shearing side of the business. He took on the manufacture of bicycles and in 1896 built his first Wolseley tricar. He went on to build another tricar – Autocar Number One – but was unable to get people to buy in to the idea, although he did eventually sell what became his first four-wheel car, the Wolseley 'Voiturette'.

When shipbuilders Vickers, Sons & Maxim approached the company with a view to taking over the car business, an agreement was put together and the Wolseley Tool and Motor Car Company of Adderley Park, Birmingham was incorporated in March 1901. Herbert Austin became managing director and by 1906 they had produced more than 1,500 cars, Wolseley in the process becoming Britain's largest motor manufacturer. After his five-year contract ended, the ambitious MD left the company to found his own car business – the world-famous Austin Motor Company Ltd.

From 1901 to 1904, Wolseley cars ranged from 5hp through to 12hp, and during 1904 there were larger models running up to 16hp, 20hp and 24hp. In 1904, Queen Alexandra

Left: A Wolseley 3.5hp, c.1901.

The Wolseley 6hp Phaeton, 1906.

bought a luxurious 5.2 litre 24hp landaulette with coil ignition, four-speed gearbox and chain drive.

Austin's post was taken by John Davenport Siddeley, and Siddeley's associate Lionel de Rothschild was brought in. Wolseley-Siddeley cars as they were now called began to outsell the old-fashioned horizontal engine cars. But the business still had to cut costs. The first factory to go was the Crayford, Kent works, which relocated to Birmingham. The London head office followed

Above: The Wolseley 14/20 of 1908.

Left: When John Davenport Siddeley joined the company, the cars were known as Wolseley-Siddeley. This is a landaulette model from 1910.

and, after heated discussions, so too did Siddeley and Rothschild in 1909.

After 1911, the cars went back to being badged as Wolseleys again and the company saw a big upward turn in profits. In 1912, the Adderley Park factory was extended. The new Stellite model was manufactured and marketed by another Vickers subsidiary, Electric and Ordnance Accessories Company Limited.

In 1913, Wolseley were back as Britain's biggest car-maker, and the following year the company was renamed Wolseley Motors Limited.

Swift Motor Company

The Coventry Sewing Machine Company was set up to import and market sewing machines from America. When their Paris agent brought a 'bone-shaker' (an early bicycle) to the factory, it signalled the start of their own bicycle-making period. In 1902, the Swift Motor Company was established. After 1907, they fitted Swift-designed engines, concentrating initially on small lightweight cars. Sadly, the company went bust in April 1931.

Left: Swift had some great successes in sporting events. Here, you can see a light model taking part in a rally during 1913 or 1914.

Right: A 1913 Swift cyclecar with its mix of car and cycle parts.

Below: The first Swift car with a Swift motorcycle just behind.

THE FIRST SWIFT CAR

Above: This 1931 Swift Cadet is believed to be the only surviving Cadet. It is a semi-fabric model which would have cost approximately £140 in its day, while a full-fabric body would have been around £160. The engine produced 8hp and was manufactured by Coventry Climax. It was the only Swift model not to use a Swift engine. It was also the last model to be made before the company went bankrupt in 1931.

Right: Even this beautiful Swallow-bodied 1931 Swift could not save the company. It is one of only two surviving (the other is in the British Motor Museum, in Gaydon, near Birmingham). It has the most successful engine they ever installed, the 1,190cc, four-cylinder, 10hp unit.

Early British Vehicles
Before World War One

The first British vehicles of the late 19th century took their lead from what was coming out of continental Europe, in particular from France and Germany. But of the 200 British makes that were launched before World War One, only half had survived, with UK vehicle production stalling at 14,000 units per annum. This figure jumped when Henry Ford opened his first factory in Manchester in 1913; with his new production methods, he instantly became the leading manufacturer of cars in the country, producing 7,310 models in his first year. World War One interrupted progress of course because car companies had to turn their skills to war work, with several also supplying vehicles to the armed forces.

A host of pedestrians, motorized vehicles, three-wheelers and horse-drawn vehicles descend on Hyde Park Corner, 1909.

Above: The 1913 AC 12hp 'Fivet', the first four-wheel model to feature a French 'Fivet' engine.

Opposite: A 1909 AC tricar.

AC Cars

The Weller brothers exhibited at the 1903 Crystal Palace Motor Show. Their financial backer, local butcher John Portwine, suggested a small three-wheeled delivery vehicle. Thus was born the Auto-Carrier of 1904. The vehicle was a success, and in 1907 a passenger version – the A, known as the AC Sociable – came into being. In 1911, the company changed its name to Auto Carriers Ltd and their first four-wheel car, of 1913, was a sporty two-seater with a gearbox on the rear axle.

The Austin Motor Company

Herbert Austin had fallen out with his employers, the Vickers brothers, over engine design and resigned his post at Wolseley where he had been remarkably successful.

Austin managed to secure backing from steel magnate Frank Kayser to start his own venture. Further assistance came from the Dunlop patent holder Harvey Du Cros and, in 1905, Austin bought an old printing works south-west of Birmingham in the small village of Longbridge. The

Below: Much activity around the first Austin car with Austin himself driving, 1906.

Below left: Austin Motors' first showroom in Long Acre, central London.

Above: The 1908 landaulette.

Left: A 1911 Austin 18/24 tourer.

Opposite: The 1912 10hp four-seater Phaeton, called 'Sirdar', came with horse-hair cushions.

following month, the Austin Motor Company Ltd was inaugurated.

Before World War One, Austin cars were generally luxury models, and the list of customers included Russian grand dukes, princesses, bishops and high officials of the Spanish government, as well as a long list of British nobility. In February 1914, Austin moved on to offer a wider selection of bodies, including tourer, limousine, landaulette and coupé styles. Engines could be provided in 15, 20, 30 and 60hp versions, with ambulances and commercial vehicles also joining the sales sheet.

Austin became a public-listed company in 1914: at that time, it probably ranked about fifth in the UK in terms of number of cars produced.

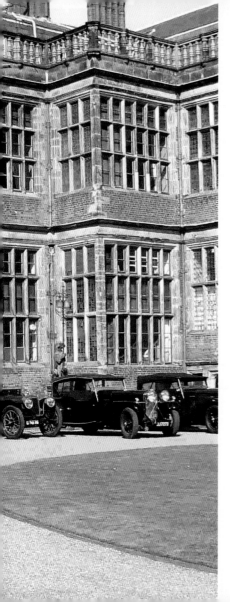

Clément-Talbot

Set up in London in 1902, the business took its name from its two directors – French car-maker Adolphe Clément and Charles Chetwynd-Talbot, 20th Earl of Shrewsbury. The earl, along with his partner D. M. Weigel, had been importing Clément cars from France, and the intention of the new company was to build cars in England.

An impressive new factory was built in Ladbroke Grove, London. It was laid out like a miniature palace with marble Ionic columns and gilded frescoes. Its stained-glass windows were etched with the Shrewsbury and Talbot coats of arms. Initially, cars were imported from France, but by 1904 they were being assembled from British-made components, except for engines which came from France.

The first wholly British car was presented in 1906, a 3.8 litre, 20/24hp, four-cylinder model. A 2.7 litre,

The AGM of the Talbot Car Club at Ingestre Hall. This 17th-century, Jacobean mansion situated near Stafford was formerly the seat of the Earls of Talbot and then the Earls of Shrewsbury.

Above: Page from the 1909 Talbot brochure.

Left: Percy Lambert in his streamlined Clément-Talbot at Brooklands, 1913.

12/16hp, four-cylinder model became available soon afterwards, and these two cars helped Talbot to establish a reputation in the market place.

In 1912, a car was specially prepared for Percy Lambert to attempt a world record run. The car was taken to Brooklands, where on 15 February 1913 Lambert became the first driver to reach 100mph.

Ford of Britain

In 1903, the first Ford cars – two model As – were imported into the UK. An enthusiastic entrepreneur by the name of Percival Perry had ordered them and, by 1911, he was selling over 400 US-built Fords per year from his offices in Shaftesbury Avenue, London. Perry realized he would have to look around for larger premises, although he did keep on his London base as a sales office.

Right: A 1908 Model T being hand-cranked.

Below: The 1911 Ford Model T complete with hood that folds back for summer driving.

Ford Motor Company (England) Ltd, forerunner of Ford of Britain, was incorporated in 1911, and that same year the first Ford factory with an assembly plant outside North America was established in an old tram factory at Trafford Park, Manchester.

Here, production of the Model T, which had had its world debut at the 1908 Olympia Motor Exhibition, began with four-man teams set up to build individual vehicles. Parts were imported from the US, although bodies were supplied individually on handcarts from a firm of body-builders called Scott Brothers located just down the road.

By 1912, Henry Ford's revolutionary introduction of the moving assembly line started, introduced progressively to Trafford Park between 1912 and 1913. This doubled output from 3,000 to 6,000 cars. By the outbreak of war in 1914, Ford sales had reached a staggering 10,000 cars per year – equal to the output of the next six biggest British manufacturers combined.

Although Henry Ford took a pacifist line during the war, the Trafford Park plant was still devoted to the production of vehicles, with an emphasis on agricultural tractors.

When hostilities ceased, the Trafford Park plant was extended and production increased to meet rising demand. Following a number of disagreements over policy, Percival Perry left the company in 1919.

Above: A busy Ford plant at Trafford Park, 1914.

Right: A 1912 Model T tourer.

53

Hillman

When Josiah Turner and James Starley set up the Coventry Sewing Machine Company, they recruited skilled engineers from London; one of the men they hired was William Hillman. The company changed its name in 1869 and began manufacturing velocipedes.

By 1885, Hillman was a partner in the Hillman, Herbert and Cooper bicycle-making company, producing a machine called the Kangaroo. Hillman was planning his next move: switching over to car production.

Above: A Hillman 25hp four-cylinder tourer, 1907. Louis Coatalen is at the wheel.

Right: Coatalen driving a Hillman-Coatalen car in the Isle of Man Tourist Trophy Race, 1914.

EARLY BRITISH VEHICLES

Hillman-Coatalen was founded in 1907 by Hillman and Breton-born Louis Coatalen. Coatalen left to join Sunbeam in 1909, and the company was re-registered as the Hillman Motor Car Company in 1910. Hillman then introduced several cars, the most popular of which was their 9hp, 1,357cc, side-valve, four-cylinder model, released in 1913.

Right: A Hillman 12–15hp model, 1909.

Below: Raymond Mays at the wheel of a Hillman Speed Model, Hertfordshire, 1921.

Humber

The Humber Cycle Company was founded by Thomas Humber in 1868. The company thrived, with factories in Coventry, Beeston and Wolverhampton. However, customers kept asking when they'd be making a motorized vehicle.

The first Humber car was produced under the guidance of Thomas Humber in 1898 and it was a three-wheel tricar – their first conventional four-wheel car had to wait until 1901 to make its bow.

A 12hp, four-cylinder model was

Above: Thomas Humber, leading the way on one of his 'Ordinary Tandem' machines, 1885.

Left: A Humber cycle factory advertisement.

Above: The 1903 Humberette – more than 30 of this model still survive today.

introduced in 1902, and 1903 saw the introduction of the Humberette, which featured a tubular frame and a 5hp, single-cylinder engine. The Humberette reappeared in 1913, but this time with an air-cooled 8hp vee-twin engine. The company also went racing, entering a three-car team in 1914 in the Tourist Trophy race. The cars were designed by F. T. Burgess and powered by 3.3 litre, four-cylinder, double-overhead-camshaft engines. World War One brought car production to an abrupt halt.

Above: Sir John Alcock and Sir Arthur Whitten Brown take delivery at the works of a new Humber 10hp in 1919 after their famous transatlantic flight. They both bought the new Humber.

Right: Up until World War One, Humber entered several works cars in competition. These included a trio of specially designed cars for the 1914 Isle of Man TT race. They were not successful in this event, but one of their drivers, W. G. Tuck, raced his TT car, along with other Humber cars, very successfully at Brooklands and in other events.

Lagonda

The Lagonda company was started by an American, Wilbur Gunn, from Ohio. He was born in 1859 and named his company after the Shawnee settlement 'Lagonda' in his native Springfield.

Gunn travelled to Britain in 1891 on family business and, while there, built a steam yacht named *Giralda*, with which he won wagers for being the fastest thing on the River Thames. He moved into motorcycle production in 1898, progressing to three-wheeler forecars made in the greenhouse of his back garden in Staines, where he was later to build a factory.

The success of these vehicles encouraged Gunn to get involved with cars and he constructed a 10hp model using parts, including the engine, from his last forecar. It wasn't long before he introduced his first proper car, launched

Left: An early Lagonda tricar, 1904–5 – these were popular, cheap to run and more comfortable than a motorcycle.

in 1907. This was a 20hp, six-cylinder Torpedo, which he raced at Brooklands and in the Moscow to St Petersburg trial of 1910. This paved the way for a healthy order book for exports to Russia. In 1913, a new light car, the 11.1hp, was presented, which used a four-cylinder, 1,099cc engine and which was fitted with the first-ever fly-off handbrake – hitherto used in racing cars. It also utilized a more advanced version of the angle iron/tinned sheet steel unitary body/

chassis systems, dispensing with the chassis frame altogether. Initially selling as a two-seater coupe, it was joined in 1914 by a four-seater.

When World War One broke out and production of cars was halted, the Staines factory began to turn out armaments, largely artillery shells.

Left: A Lagonda light car, the 11.1hp, was introduced in 1913, featuring a four-cylinder engine. This one is from 1914.

Below: Gunn introduced his first proper car in 1907, the 20hp, six-cylinder model. It also raced and seen here is an example at the St Petersburg Motor Show in 1910.

Morgan

Henry Frederick Stanley Morgan, widely known as 'HFS', was the son and grandson of a vicar, but he did not follow in their footsteps. Instead, he turned his thoughts to designing what became one of the most individual cars in British motoring history, the Morgan.

Born in 1884, he started work as an employee of the Great Western Railway (GWR). He left GWR in 1904 and in 1905 opened a garage in Malvern Link, Worcestershire, selling Darracq and Wolseley cars.

In 1909, Morgan bought a twin-cylinder Peugeot engine intended for use in a motorcycle design, but a last-minute change of mind saw him construct a car. Help came via William Stephenson-Peach, who was the engineering master at Malvern College, where Morgan was given the run of a well-equipped workshop.

The car, a three-wheel, single-seater, went into production at the newly established Morgan Motor Co. Ltd, with

Left: A 1914 Sporting Runabout with JAP engine. The first Runabout was produced in 1910 with a Peugeot engine.

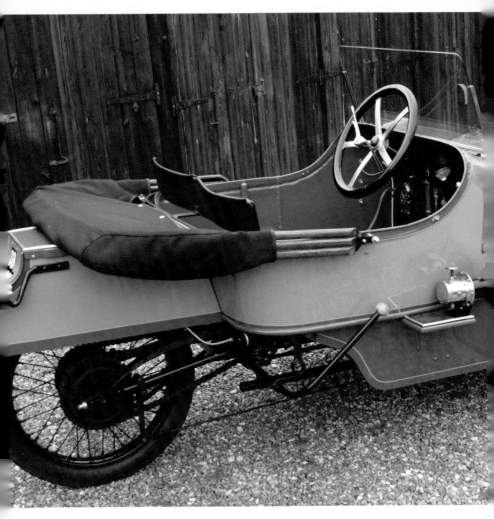

Left: The three-wheeler was equipped with a two-forward-speed gearbox but had no reverse.

Right: With the engine cover lifted up, the JAP, side-valve, air-cooled 964cc engine could easily be viewed.

premises in Malvern Link. It was a small-scale operation. At the 1910 Olympia Motor Show in London, three single-seater, 964cc JAP-engine models went on show.

Morgan decided to create two-seater models to meet the demands of the market. These were built in 1911 and an agency was taken up by Harrods department store in London; the Morgan thus became the only car ever to appear in a shop window at Harrods. Before World War One, Morgan launched a racing model based on the Grand Prix chassis and using a MAG engine.

Left: A line-up of Morris Oxford cars outside the Morris works, Oxford, 1913.

Right: The first production model: this design, in gestation as the Morris Oxford light car since 1910, was completed by late 1912.

William Richard Morris Motors

After leaving school at the age of 15, William Morris became an apprentice with a company that sold and repaired bicycles. Unhappy at being denied a wage rise, he started his own business just one year later in a shed at the rear of his parents' house in Oxford.

This was a roaring success and he soon opened a shop where he not only repaired bicycles but assembled them

too, inscribing them with a gilt cycle wheel and the name 'The Morris'.

By 1901, he was making motorcycles and also running a taxi service. He also sold, repaired and hired cars. In 1910 he moved into much bigger premises.

In 1913, WRM Motors produced its first car, the Morris Oxford. Using bought-in components, he assembled the car at a disused military training college near Cowley. 1915 saw the introduction of the Morris Cowley model.

The Morris Oxford was assembled rather than manufactured, using parts from well-known suppliers of the period.

Riley

In 1890, William Riley bought
the Bonnick Cycle Company of
Coventry, changing its name
to the Riley Cycle Company
in 1896. Percy Riley, middle
son of William, left school and
secretly began experimenting
with cars, making his first light
two-seater in 1898 at the age of
16. Little is known about that
car, but the engine featured the

Right: The 5hp Riley Popular tricar.

*Below: A 1907 Riley 9hp with the world's
first standardized detachable road wheels.*

0 WY-29

E ROAD

first mechanically operated inlet-valve system. In 1902 three Riley brothers, Victor, Percy and Allan, borrowed capital from their mother and set up their own company, the Riley Engine Company, Coventry.

When the younger Riley brothers, Stanley and Cecil, left school they joined their fellow siblings in the enterprise, which concentrated on turning out the 12/18 V-twin, and the 17/30 four-cylinder cars.

In 1913 Stanley took over the Nero Engine Company, originally founded by Victor Riley, and decided to build a new 10hp, four-cylinder car, filling the gap in the market that wasn't covered by the other Riley cars. A prototype appeared in 1914, but by now companies were required to supply materials for the war effort.

Left: The chauffeur to Lord William Beveridge stands proudly next to his Riley 12/18, c.1910.

Above: The Riley 9hp, V-twin, 1907 model.

This 1904 Royce is one of three cars built at Cook St, Manchester.

Inset opposite right: The 1905 model.

Rolls-Royce

Charles Stewart Rolls was born in 1877, third son of Lord and Lady Llangattock, in Berkeley Square in the heart of London. He went to school at Eton and studied mechanical engineering at Trinity College, Cambridge. He was the first undergraduate to own a car.

After university, and already an accomplished motorist, he broke the land speed record in Dublin, driving a 30hp Mors at nearly 83mph. Sadly, because the timing

79

A Rolls-Royce about to negotiate one of the tight corners at the 1906 Tourist Trophy on the Isle of Man.

equipment was not approved by the governing body, the record was never acknowledged. Rolls set up a car dealership, one of the first in Britain, with his friend Claude Johnson. C. S. Rolls & Co. imported and sold Peugeot and Minerva cars from France and Belgium respectively.

Henry Royce's start in life couldn't have been more different. He was born in Peterborough in 1863 and sent out to work at the age of nine. When he was 14, one of his aunts paid for him to start an apprenticeship with the Great Northern Railway Works. In the evenings, he studied algebra, French and electrical engineering.

He managed to secure a job with the Electric Light and Power Company. But his true ambition was to be an engineer and he started an electrical business with his friend Ernest Claremont, a fellow engineer. Royce also patented improvements he made to the bayonet light bulb.

Royce bought himself a second-hand, two-cylinder Decauville. Having found faults in the car, he was determined to improve on them, and it was this attitude that eventually led to the Rolls-Royce philosophy of 'Take the best and make it

A 20hp Rolls-Royce from 1905–6.

better'. By the end of 1903, Royce had designed and built his first petrol engine and in April 1904 he drove his Royce 10hp motor car into his local town.

Henry Edmunds, not only a shareholder in Royce's company but also a friend of Rolls, couldn't stop talking about the new 10hp car. He mentioned it to Rolls who at the time was frustrated by the fact that he could only sell foreign imports.

He wanted a great British car he could sell.

Rolls and Royce met on 4 May 1904 in Manchester and, within minutes of clapping eyes on the 10hp car, Rolls knew he had found what he needed. He took the car for a spin and agreed on the spot that he would sell as many cars as Royce could build – under the name of Rolls-Royce.

In 1907, the incredible Silver Ghost was introduced, a car that became the basis for the marque's legendary status. It competed in the 1913 Alpine Trial, a 14,371-mile slog through some of the toughest mountain terrain in Europe. The car provided such a level of comfort and reliability that critics quickly acquiesced in naming it 'The Best Car in the World'.

By the end of 1907, the Silver Ghost production line was running

Above: The beautiful 1907 Rolls-Royce Silver Ghost with its Barker 4/5 seater touring body.

T. E. Lawrence, probably better known as Lawrence of Arabia, in his Silver Ghost in 1916.

at four chassis per week and their order books were full. There was a need for more space, and so a modern factory was built on a 12-acre site in Derby. Production of the Silver Ghost at the new factory rose to seven chassis per week and remained that way until 1914. Rolls-Royces were selling like hot cakes.

83

Seen here is a Rover 8hp model of 1904.

Rover

The Rover Company was founded by John Kemp Starley and William Sutton in 1878. Starley had previously worked with his uncle James Starley – known as the father of the cycle trade – who began by manufacturing sewing machines and then switched to bicycles in 1869; it seems a well-worn track. The first use of the name Rover was on a bicycle manufactured by Starley & Sutton Co. of Coventry in 1884.

Starley died before he could finish

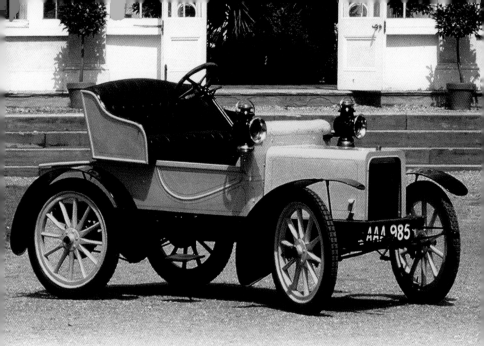

The 1906 model with 6hp.

his work on motorcycles, but new managing director Harry Smith introduced the first 2.75hp Rover motorcycle in 1902. Work on these had ceased by 1905 as the team prepared to move into cars.

Smith hired Edmund Lewis, an ex-Daimler employee, to design a light car, which was presented in 1904 as the 8hp Rover. This used a conventional front-mounted 1,327cc, single-cylinder engine, but the chassis was unusual in that it had a steel backbone frame. A smaller 780cc, 6hp model joined it soon after. This featured a more conventional wood-and-flitch plate chassis. This became the template for a couple of cars to come – the four-cylinder 16/20hp of 1905, and

The Rover 12hp landaulette, 1912.

the two-cylinder 12hp of 1908.

Lewis left Rover in 1905, and was succeeded by Owen Clegg, an ex-Wolseley–Siddleley employee, in 1910. In 1906, the Rover Motor Company Ltd was formed. The first important model was the Twelve, designed by Clegg. The car used an L-head, mono-block, four-cylinder engine and was made from 1912 until 1924. A model Eighteen was also available based along similar lines, but it never proved as popular.

During World War One, Rover produced mortars, gas shells and fuses, along with Maudslay three-ton lorries and Sunbeam 16hp staff cars.

Singer

George Singer founded Singer & Co. in 1874. The first four-wheel car, introduced in 1905, was made under licence from Lea Francis and designed by Alexander Craig.

By 1906, Singer had designed their own car. The following year they introduced a range of two-, three- and four-cylinder models using mainly White and Poppe engines, although the larger 2.4 litre and 3.7

Left: The Singer tricars of 1905 were powered by either a 6hp or a 9hp, water-cooled engine produced by Riley.

Above: A family and their chauffeur pose for a photograph next to their 1913 Singer landaulette.

litre engines were sourced from Aster.

The company went into receivership in 1908. It was reformed as Singer and Co. (1909), and a 2.5 litre Sixteen with three-speed gearbox was introduced. 1911 saw the arrival of the L-head, 2.6

litre and 3.3 litre cars, with the bigger cars boasting worm drive and Sankey detachable steel wheels.

The Ten arrived in 1912, and used a four-cylinder, 1,100cc engine with three-speed gearbox; this was seen as the first modern baby car.

Standard

Reginald W. Maudslay, born in 1871, was the great grandson of the pioneering engineer Henry Maudslay. He went to work for Sir John Wolfe-Barry, designer of Tower Bridge, who gave him £3,000 to help set up the Standard Motor Company in 1903.

Alexander Craig was given the position of works manager and designer.

The first car was a single-cylinder model with three-speed gearbox and shaft-drive to the rear wheels. This was initially replaced by a two-cylinder car, and not long afterwards by three- and four-cylinder versions.

Right: Standard went through a phase of naming their cars after towns, for example the car shown is a Standard 'Coleshill', a market town in north Warwickshire. For a small 9hp, two-door model, it came very well equipped.

Left: Standard's first light car was the Model S, launched in 1913.

Below: This is a rare sketch. Marked January 1903, it was an original design done by Maudslay, even before the company had come into being.

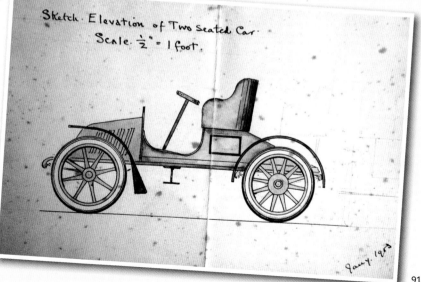

Sketch. Elevation of Two Seated Car.
Scale. ½" = 1 foot.

Jany 1903

91

Inset: This car dates to c.1909 and shows Maudslay at the wheel. It could be his personal car, the one that was later turned into a pick-up for use around the works – this apparently survived into World War Two.

Left: An early Standard, c.1905, again with Maudslay driving. It shows the early radiator, before the familiar shouldered version came in after 1906.

Maudslay drove the first Standard car to compete in the RAC Tourist Trophy in 1905. By 1911, the 8hp model was being produced in large numbers and the general range of cars had become comprehensive. Seventy four-cylinder, 16hp cars, including some unusual 4 x 4s, were supplied for King George V and his entourage, including the Viceroy of India, for the 1911 Delhi Durbar.

John Marston   *Louis Coatalen*   *Thomas Cureton*

Sunbeam

John Marston was the son of a landowner. Educated in London, he became an apprentice at the Edward Perry tinplate works in Wolverhampton, and aged just 23 he bought two other tinplate manufacturers in nearby Bilston and set up his own business. When Perry died, Marston also bought out his business and continued working from there, incorporating bicycle production into the schedules.

Thomas Cureton was an apprentice with Marston, and the two started work on a prototype motor car, producing experimental machines

The second car built by Sunbeam, 1904.

The first production car branded 'Sunbeam' designed by Maxwell Mabberly-Smith.

1903 Sunbeam.

between 1899 and 1901.

The first production models adopted a strange format – often known as diamond-wheel layout – with seats that faced outwards. The design was the work of Maxwell Mabberly-Smith and, featuring a De Dion 2¾hp engine, they were called Sunbeam Mableys.

Thomas Charles Willis Pullinger, who was involved in the bicycle trade, rode to the Sunbeam works in Wolverhampton in 1902 on a quadricycle that he had built himself.

97

*Coatalen's first Sunbeam was the
14/20, with shaft-driven rear axle.*

Asked to prepare a blueprint for success, he suggested the company start by buying whole cars from an established manufacturer. In time, they could buy cars without certain components, which they would then make themselves, finally buying in only the engine because they would be able to manufacture everything else themselves.

In this way, rights were obtained for the 12hp Berliet, which were sold as Sunbeams from 1903. As suggested, complete chassis were imported initially, but later imports were confined to just the engine and gearbox. In 1905, the motor department at Sunbeam was separated from the rest and named the Sunbeam Motor Car Company Ltd. Within two years, it had spread across two acres of factory space and was producing an all-British 16/20 designed by Angus Shaw.

Louis Coatalen joined Sunbeam in 1909 and became chief designer. He organized production, so that all parts were now built in-house. He introduced his first design, the 14/20, which was the first model to have shaft drive to the rear axle. In 1910, he built the Sunbeam Nautilus, his first dedicated land-speed-record car, but sadly because of engineering problems it was abandoned.

A racing programme was also instigated to pull in publicity. Company profits rose from a mere £90 in 1909 to a staggering £95,000 in 1913, and 2,400 workers were taken on. With the outbreak of World War One, Sunbeam started producing materials for the war.

The Nautilus, 1910, powered by a 4.2 litre engine.

Vauxhall

Founded by Scottish
marine engineer Alexander
Wilson, Alex Wilson and
Company built high-
pressure steam engines,
as well as compound and
triple-expansion engines for
tugboats.

In 1894 Wilson left the
company and the name was
changed to the Vauxhall
Iron Works Company Ltd.
The new chief engineer,
F. W. Hodges, designed the
first petrol-engine car, which
was presented in 1903.

That first car featured
a 5hp, single-cylinder,
water-cooled engine, had
two forward gears with no
reverse and came equipped
with tiller steering. The
following year, it was given
a proper steering wheel,
a reverse gear and a 6hp
engine. In 1905, part of the
business moved to Luton.

*The second car to be produced by
Vauxhall was the 1904 6hp model.*

Marine engines continued to be made alongside a smattering of cars.

Laurence Pomeroy moved to Vauxhall in 1905 as assistant to chief engineer Frederick Hodges.

Pomeroy's first design, the Y-type Y1, was incredibly successful at the 1908 RAC and Scottish 2,000 Mile Reliability Trials. The company decided to put it into production, initially known as the A09 car, later to become the Vauxhall A-type.

Four distinct versions were produced. The A-type Vauxhall became one of the most acclaimed 3 litre cars of its day. Later, the 4 litre D-type was converted as a staff car during the war; one of these cars was the first to cross the Rhine after the signing of the Armistice.

Left: The Vauxhall D-type army staff car: this is a 1918 version.

Right: This Prince Henry three-door, Sports Torpedo has a body by Hoskison of Birmingham.

Below: The C-class, better known as the Prince Henry, was made between 1911 and 1913.

Between the Wars
1919 to 1939

After 1918 – with the advent of mass production pioneered by Henry Ford – there was a boom in private car ownership, despite the Wall Street Crash of 1929. But it had always been a case of survival of the fittest. In 1922, there were 183 companies producing cars in the UK, a figure which plummeted to just 58 by 1929.

Private car ownership doubled during the 1930s and, by the end of the decade, there were two million cars on UK roads. In 1932, taking over from the French, the UK became Europe's largest producer. Shapes and sizes were changing, with motorists now looking for more style from their transport, and so features like sloping windscreens, sweeping wings, pillarless windows and rounded roofs came in, along with numerous technical advances.

Westminster Bridge c.1915—1923.

AC Cars

In 1918, a new car was announced, based on a pre-war design and fitted with a French Fivet engine. The plan had been to fit a six-cylinder engine, but because of finances the offer of an off-the-peg alternative was too good to turn down.

With the upturn, AC put in an order for 2,000 British Anzani, 1,496cc, four-cylinder, side-valve, 11.9hp engines in 1919. Later that year, the 1½ litre, six-cylinder engine was also announced, which went up a size in 1922 – to 1,991cc.

S. F. Edge acquired the company outright in 1927 and reregistered it as AC (Acedes) Ltd. As the Depression began to grip, the company went into voluntary liquidation in 1929; production ceased for a time before it was sold on to the Hurlock brothers, William and Charles.

Right: The AC 12hp Six, 1925.

Above: The 1934 AC Ace 16–66hp Long Greyhound.

Right: A 1936 AC 16–80hp two-seater Competition Sports – ex-Betty Haig car-class winner, 1946 Alpine Rally.

The brothers did not intend to become car-makers; they just wanted to use the factory space as a depot. But a small trickle of specially made cars appeared between 1930 and 1933, and they began building attractive bodies in-house, leading to a new range of models in 1932. Production was on a small scale, though, and the final car was released in 1940.

Aston Martin

Robert Bamford and Lionel Martin were partners in a car business in Chelsea. They sold Singer cars and serviced GWs and Calthorpes; Martin regularly entered cars in the Aston Hill Climb in Buckinghamshire.

Robert Bamford

In 1914, Martin put together a hybrid competition car with a 1,400cc, four-cylinder, Coventry-Simplex engine, fitted to a 1908 Grand Prix des Voiturettes Isotta-Fraschini. He gave it the name Aston Martin due to his success at the Aston Hill Climb.

Lionel Martin

After the war, the company moved to Kensington. Bamford left to start his own successful business and, in 1922, Aston Martin competed in the French Grand Prix.

The Aston Martin 1.5 litre tourer, 1928.

Above: The 2 litre Speed model, 1937.

Left: The beautiful Aston Martin 1.5 litre Mk II, 1934.

In 1926, Bill Renwick, Augustus (Bert) Bertelli and a group of investors took control and renamed it Aston Martin Motors Ltd. Models came thick and fast off the production line. Bertelli introduced a number of models: the 1½ litre T-type, International, Le Mans, Mk II, the Ulster, a 2 litre 15/98 and the racing version the 'Speed Model'. At the 1933 Le Mans race, the 1½ litre model made a clean sweep of the podium places within its class.

113

Austin

After the war, Herbert Austin decided on a one-model policy, with the 20hp, 3,620cc engine the common denominator, but in 1921 the company went into receivership. A financial restructuring breathed life back into the company. New financial director Ernest Payton played a critical role in the recovery, and Carl Engelbach was brought in as the new works director. Smaller cars were introduced, the 1,661cc

Above: The Austin Seven was one of the most popular cars ever produced. It was made under licence in several countries.

Left: The Austin range received a make-over in 1934 and the Seven gained the designation Mk II. With a whole new look, it stayed in production until 1939.

Twelve in 1922 and the little Seven later that year, both aimed at the mass market. The Seven was also built in several other countries under licence. All-steel bodies, Girling brakes and synchromesh gears were part of the formula for success.

Austin made cars during World War Two, alongside trucks and aircraft, including the Lancaster bomber of 617 Squadron – the 'Dambusters'!

Bentley

Although the first Bentley car was not produced until 1921, Walter Owen Bentley and his brother Horace Milner Bentley were already selling imported French models from Doriot, Flandrin & Parant (DFP) in Cricklewood, north London. But 'WO', as he was known, was keen to build his own car. One day at the DFP factory, he noticed an aluminium paperweight on his desk, which gave him the idea of replacing cast-iron engine parts with aluminium. The first Bentley aluminium pistons were used in Sopwith Camels.

Captain Woolf 'Babe' Barnato acquired his first Bentley in 1925 and had some success racing at Brooklands. In 1926, he became the proud owner of Bentley after a lengthy period of financial wrangling.

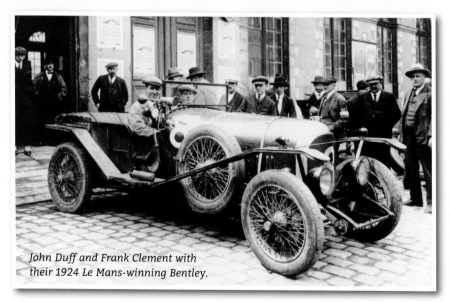

John Duff and Frank Clement with their 1924 Le Mans-winning Bentley.

The legendary 'Bentley Boys' were a group of wealthy motoring enthusiasts all of whom favoured Bentley cars. They also helped to keep the high-performance reputation of the cars alive. Bentley cars won the 24 Hour Le Mans race consecutively between 1927 and 1930.

In 1930, Barnato and his 6½ litre Speed Six took 'Le Train Bleu' (The Blue Train) challenge; racing the train from Cannes to Calais, before crossing the Channel and heading for London, beating the train to the capital. Later that year, he took delivery of another Speed Six which had a streamlined fastback 'Sportsman Coupe' by Gurney Nutting; these cars became known as the 'Blue Train Bentleys'.

Above: 1928: Race winners Woolf Barnato and Bernard Rubin with their 4½ litre Bentley.

Right: The Bentley 3 litre, generally seen as the sports car that put Bentley on the map in 1919.

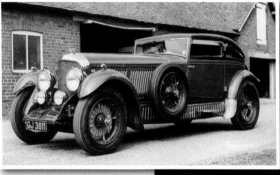

*Above: The 1929 Bentley
Speed Six, Blue Train Special.*

In 1930, a new 8 litre model was introduced, but the Great Depression killed off demand for expensive cars. Rolls-Royce stepped in to save Bentley. The 1933 3½ litre Bentley was a sporting variant of the Rolls-Royce 20/50 and it was advertised as 'the silent sports car', a slogan Rolls-Royce continued to use for Bentley cars.

Below: A beautiful 1930 Bentley 8 litre.

Clément-Talbot

George Roesch's first design after the war was the 12hp A12 prototype of 1919, but it never reached production because the company was taken over by Société Alexandre Darracq. Shortly afterwards, they also bought Sunbeam to create the STD group; its engineering department was headed up by Louis Coatalen.

Pre-war 15/20hp and 25/50hp models were revived, alongside a 1 litre 8/18hp model in 1921. It was not long before Clément-Talbot ran into

Right: Tim Rose-Richards and Owen Saunders-Davies in the Talbot 105 Team Car, in which they came third in the 1931 Le Mans 24 Hour race. They were only beaten by supercharged Alfa Romeo and Mercedes cars.

Inset top: The 1928 Talbot 14/45 tourer. The tourer saved Clément Talbot Ltd in 1926.

financial problems. Roesch was recalled to save the company, and in 1926 they launched the 1,666cc, 14/45hp, six-cylinder model. It was roomy and inexpensive and with its many modern features helped the company to survive.

Seen here outside Ingestre Hall,
Staffordshire is a most beautiful 1936
Talbot BI 105 Speed Saloon.

Ford

The year 1922 saw sales fall behind Morris for the first time. Although the Manchester plant was well served, Ernest C. Kanzler decided on a new plot – Dagenham in Essex. The first vehicles to be built there were a model AA 1.5 ton truck and a Model A car in 1931. Perry, who had been ill, was invited back to Ford by Henry Ford himself in 1928, and in 1932 Trafford Park closed, having produced 250,000 Model Ts and 14,000 Model As.

With the Depression hitting hard, a new smaller model was needed. Enter the Model Y in 1932, and, between 1932 and 1937, the Dagenham and Cork factories turned out 157,000 of those.

Above: Ford introduced automobile mass production in 1913 at the first Ford plant in Highland Park, Michigan.

Right: Henry Ford with a 1927 Ford Model T.

Top: A Rootes showroom full of Hillman and Humber models.

Left: A Hillman Minx saloon in Auckland, New Zealand.

Opposite top: The Aero Minx, with its slightly Art Deco look.

Hillman

After the war, the 11hp Peace model went on sale as a two- or four-seater tourer, or two-seater drophead coupé. Between 1920 and 1922, the Hillman Super Sports model was introduced, of which only about 120 were made because of its high price.

The 11hp model was in production until 1925, when a new model, the Fourteen, was presented. This had a

1,954cc, four-cylinder engine. It sold well and, in 1927, the factory expanded – by now it was making its own bodies too.

The Rootes Brothers took on distribution rights and soon Hillman, Humber and Commer Commercial Vehicles came under the control of the Rootes family. In 1931, a return to the side-valve engine saw the six-cylinder Wizard introduced, and not long afterwards the first Minx. The Wizard 65 and 75 were replaced by the Hillman 16hp and 20/70 models until 1936, when the new Sixteen, Hawk and 80 came in.

Humber

After the war Humber reintroduced the 10 and 14 models, with the latter being given a larger 15.9hp engine. By 1923 these had been joined by the 8/18, 985cc model.

In 1925, Humber purchased Commercial Cars Ltd, of Luton, followed by Hillman in 1928. In 1932 Rootes took control of Humber. The new and cheaper-to-build side-valve engine replaced the inlet-over-exhaust (ioe) unit, and during the 1930s numerous rationalizations were brought in.

But the classic cars of this period were the Snipe saloon and Pullman limousine. Between 1938 and 1939, a Super Snipe model was produced for World War Two – probably the most famous was used by Viscount Montgomery and known as 'Old Faithful'.

Right: The 1931 model 16/50 tourer. Humber had changed their radiator shape and started updating models as styles changed from 'vintage', that is 1920s, into 1930s-type coachwork.

Lagonda

Lagonda benefitted from expansion during the war years and afterwards production remained steady, with the 11.1 growing into the 12/24 which lasted until 1926. A new and more expensive 14/60 was also introduced, which featured a new four-cylinder, twin-camshaft engine.

The 14/60 was renamed the 2 litre in 1928, and a speed model was introduced to keep everyone on their toes. 1928 also saw a new 2 litre, six-cylinder model, and a supercharged 2 litre model came in 1930. Difficulties with the 3 litre gearbox were overcome by the introduction of a new model, the Selector Special, which used a new vacuum-operated, eight-speed, pre-selector gearbox.

Both pages: The 1936 Lagonda M45 Rapide, which the company announced as 'the fastest car in the world'. The controls could be found on the steering wheel.

The Depression hit Lagonda hard during the early 1930s, and in 1932 a new 2 litre, six-cylinder model, with a brought-in engine from Crossley was introduced. The following year, two new models were released, the 9hp Rapier with new 1,104cc, twin overhead-camshaft engine designed by Tim Ashcroft, and the M45 4½ litre, six-cylinder model featuring a Meadows engine. This came in a variety of body styles.

During the mid-1930s, Lagonda found they had financial problems, too many chassis on their hands and not enough sales. A receiver was called in and tenders were invited; the highest bidder was Alan Good, who renamed the company Lagonda Motors (Staines) Ltd. W. O. Bentley was brought in by Good to modify the M45 which then became the LG45.

Left: The 1935 Lagonda M45 drophead.

Cecil Kimber at the wheel of the first real MG sports car 'Old Number One' in 1925.

Opposite: The 1927 MG 'Old Speckled Hen'.

MG

Cecil Kimber was manager of Morris Garages in 1922, but he was tired of selling just the Oxford and Cowley models. So he ordered some Cowley chassis and fitted a body to them, made for him by Carbodies of Coventry, and sold them under the Chummy name. Initially he assembled them at Morris Garages in Longwall Street, but soon moved into a small workshop in Alfred Lane.

A further model followed, a two-seater with a Raworth (Oxford) body, of which only six were made. A four-seater model fitted to an Oxford chassis, and advertised in the

Above: An 18/80 from 1928 – the first 'real' MG.

Morris Owner magazine as the MG V-front saloon, was presented in 1924. A one-off special was made for Cecil Kimber in 1925, traditionally known as 'Old Number One', which featured a four-cylinder, 1,496cc engine.

Although they had only shifted premises two years earlier, by 1927 a further move was needed, financed by William Morris, to a new factory in Edmund Road. The familiar bullnose radiator

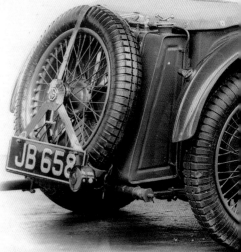

was now replaced by a new flat-style radiator.

In 1927, the company became Morris Garages and a limited company followed shortly afterwards in 1928 as the MG Car Company. During 1927, the MG name secured its first racing victory in Buenos Aires. As MG became more self-sufficient, they looked beyond Morris for their components, buying frames, engines and axles from their own suppliers.

MG had their first stand at the 1928 Olympia show, where they exhibited the M-type, which featured an 847cc overhead-camshaft (OHC) engine, and the 18/80 Six, which used a six-cylinder engine with OHC. With these new models, sales and production increased dramatically.

The 1929 MG Six, as it was first known, was introduced at the 1928 Motor Show.

A final move was made in 1929 to premises in Abingdon, outside Oxford.

The company was reaping the rewards of its outstanding competition department. The K3 Magnette achieved many victories. But racing was a costly business and after pressure from Morris, Kimber severed his connection with Carbodies and Morris Bodies.

William Morris became Lord Nuffield in 1934 and the following year he sold the MG Car Company to his own Morris Motors. He brought in Lord Leonard as managing director, who promptly closed down the competition

A 1934 MG P-type with modified C-type body, seen at speed at Loton Park in 2012.

department. OHC engines were replaced by pushrod units, the TA model was given a 1,292cc engine and a new model was presented to rival the newly announced SS Jaguar, the SA 2 litre, which used a Wolseley Super Six engine.

When World War Two started, car production ceased and the company concentrated on war work. Kimber had secured a contract to build the front section of the Albemarle bomber, but failed to mention this to anybody and was dismissed in 1941.

Morgan

Morgan benefitted from war work, and, when hostilities ceased, a family four-seater was the first model out of the factory gate. Further premises were also acquired in Pickersleigh Road in 1919, with full production moving there in 1923.

The three-wheelers were selling well and also winning lots of competitions. The road-going versions were upgraded with more powerful V-twin engines, nicer bodywork, front-wheel brakes and electric starting. Engines varied between Anzani, Precision, Blackburn and, of course, JAP. A four-cylinder, three-wheeler went

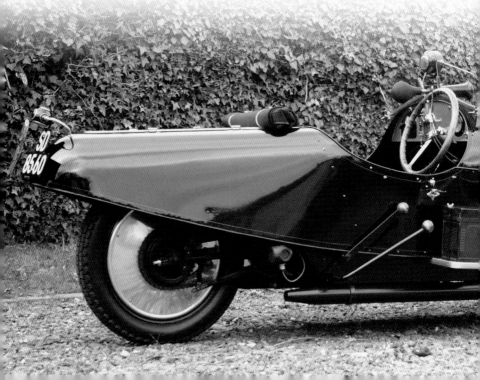

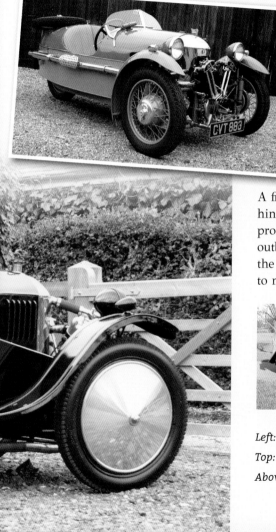

on sale in 1933, which used an 8hp Ford engine; Matchless engines were now available too, due to a shortage of JAP units.

In 1935, Morgan presented their first four-wheel model, the 4/4, with a 1,122cc Coventry Climax engine. A fire broke out at the factory, hindering but not stopping production of cars. However, the outbreak of World War Two did, the factory now turning its hand to making aircraft parts.

Left: 1924 Aero with Blackburn engine.

Top: A Morgan Super Sport of 1934.

Above: The first four-wheel 4/4, 1935.

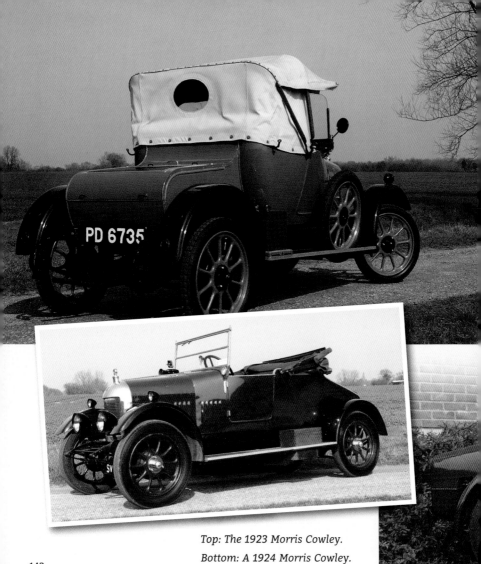

Top: The 1923 Morris Cowley.

Bottom: A 1924 Morris Cowley.

Morris

At the start of the war in 1914 Morris travelled to the USA to find cheaper components. Three thousand engines were ordered from the Continental Motor Manufacturing Company of Detroit. Sadly, half the engines were lost at sea.

The Morris Cowley was introduced in 1915, but production was interrupted because of the war. Once hostilities ceased, production resumed, with cars now using Hotchkiss-supplied engines.

Morris went with a two-model policy and, alongside the Cowley, came a better-equipped Oxford model, selling for £50 more.

A slump hit sales dramatically during 1921, but Morris decided to reduce prices. The strategy worked and sales soared. The year 1919 saw just 400 cars leave the production line, but by 1925 that had risen to a staggering 56,000. During this period, Morris bought factories in Abingdon, Birmingham and Swindon to add to the Oxford plants.

Morris bought out Hotchkiss and renamed the company Morris

The Morris Red Flash had a top speed of 80mph.

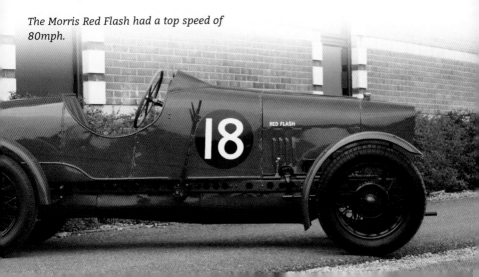

Engines Ltd. Back-axle suppliers E. G. Wrigley & Co. found themselves in financial trouble, so Morris took them over, repeating the feat with SU Carburettors in 1926.

The 'flatnose' radiators arrived in 1926, taking the place of the familiar 'bullnose' type and in 1927, Morris bought Wolseley Motors. Morris introduced a 2½ litre six-cylinder Six in 1928 and the Morris Minor in 1929, a small car with an 847cc engine.

The Minor, intended as a rival to the Austin Seven, never really sold well and was succeeded by the Morris Eight. The Morris Major followed in 1931, and the Fifteen Six in 1935.

In 1935 after the factory had been modernized, the model Eight became a best-seller as a two- and four-door saloon, and the series II 10hp and 12hp

Right: The 1926 Morris Oxford.

models were launched with fastback-style bodywork, to be followed shortly by the 16hp, 18hp and 21hp, with similar styling. The Series III models followed in 1938 and, later that year, the integral construction Series M Ten saloon was presented, followed by the re-bodied Series E Eight. That same year, Morris acquired the bankrupt Riley and Autovia companies.

To mark his achievements, William Morris was made a baronet in 1929, a baron in 1934, and in 1938 Viscount Nuffield. The one-millionth Morris was made in 1939, and so Cowley became the first British factory to reach the million-car mark. But once again war broke out in Europe and the company turned to making armaments.

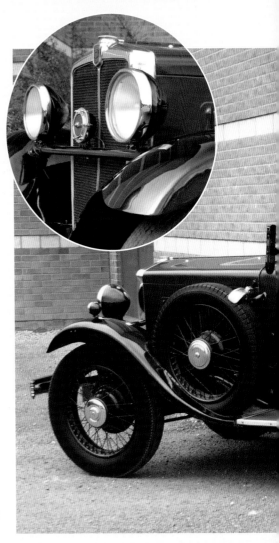

The new 'flat nose' Morris replaced the traditional 'bullnose' in 1926.

146

Riley

After the war, a new 10.8hp model, designed by Harry Rush, was launched. Made by Riley (Coventry) Ltd, it was given a larger-capacity 11.9hp engine in 1925. These were successful for the company and the Redwing model also gained good competition results. The Riley Nine came

in 1926 and its engine featured inclined overhead valves, operated by twin camshafts.

The new 1,496cc engine of 1936 powered a variety of models: Merlin, Kestrel and Falcon saloons, Lynx sports/tourer and the two-seater sports Sprite. The MPH, derived from the 1933 Tourist Trophy cars, was a short-lived, six-cylinder sports model, much like the 2,178cc, 90-degree, V8 engine 8/90 introduced in 1936.

By 1937, things looked bleak for Riley, what with the unsuccessful V8 models, the lack of a general manager, and all the unsold cars that had piled up in the factory yard. In short, sales had stagnated. Even the appointment of a new manager did not help and in 1938

the receiver was called in. Later that year, both Riley companies were bought by Lord Nuffield for incorporation into Morris Motors Ltd.

Riley (Coventry) Successors Ltd was created and Victor Riley was appointed managing director. Although 1939 saw a new range of cars using the 12/4 and 16/4 (Big Four) engines, few were sold before war work commenced in 1940.

Following World War Two, the RM series was launched with the 12/4

Left: The 1932 March Special.

Below: A 1924 Riley Redwing.

engine, joined in 1947 by a 2.4 litre Big Four. Riley left Coventry in 1948 and moved to Abingdon to share the MG factory, which meant a steady loss of identity for both as they merged into the British Motor Corporation range.

The 2.4 litre RM was replaced by the Pathfinder in 1924 and the RMF, last of the RM series, was made in 1955. The Riley name survived until 1969 and could be found on several BMC cars.

The Riley MPH, manufactured 1934–35.

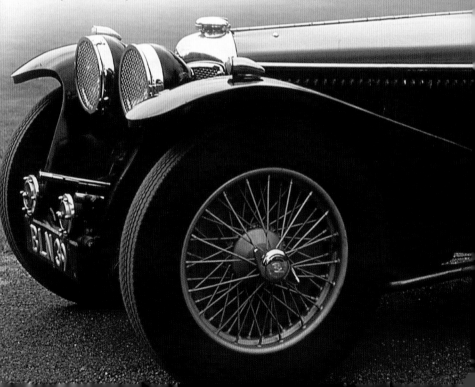

Rolls-Royce

After the war, Rolls-Royce announced a new car, which although frowned upon as a departure from the norm, became known as the 'Baby Rolls'. The Twenty was aimed at owner-drivers, but many were sold to customers with chauffeurs. The 20/25 model followed and used a 3,669cc engine with various body styles.

The legendary Silver Ghost name was phased out in 1925 and replaced by New Phantom, later to become simply Phantom I, and incorporating an overhead-valve engine. The Phantom II followed in 1929 and later still the Phantom III, the first-ever Rolls-Royce with a

Right: HRH The Prince of Wales is seen in a 1919 40/50 Silver Ghost on a visit to India.

Below: The 1937 Rolls-Royce Sedanca De Ville 25/30.

V-12 engine, in 1936.

Sir Henry Royce died in 1933 but not before receiving a baronetcy. 1938 saw the Wraith model, which was built at the Derby factory and supplied with chassis only to independent coachbuilders.

With the arrival of World War Two, Rolls-Royce concentrated on the manufacture of their Merlin aircraft engine.

Rover

In 1920 the 14hp, 998cc Eight was introduced. Two lines of development followed, the smaller cars like the Eight and its successors, the water-cooled, four-cylinder 9/20 and 10/25, and the solid middle of the range 14/45 and 16/50. Their lack of success meant the company had to change. The 1,410cc Pilot followed, and things improved: the 10hp, 12hp, 14hp, 16hp and 20hp models of the 1930s established foundations for the future.

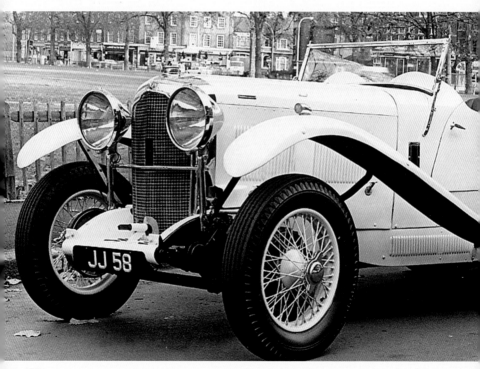

Top: The 1937 Rover 16 family car.

Above: The 1921 Rover 8, their first production vehicle.

Left: The short-lived 2 or 2.5 litre 1927 Rover Meteor 20.

Singer

After World War One was over, Singer continued to produce the Ten, which sold at the rate of around 50 to 60 per week. William Rootes started as an apprentice with Singer and turned into a very successful salesman.

A 2 litre Fifteen was presented in 1921, the same year that they bought the Coventry Premier Motorcycle Company, and in 1926 they also acquired the Calcott factory. The Ten, now available as the Senior and the Junior – and the first cheap British car with overhead-camshaft engine – completed the range.

Above: The 1929 Singer Junior.

Right: The 1933 Singer 9 Sports Coupé.

In 1927, the company moved into additional premises in Birmingham. Unlike many other car companies, Singer made nearly all its own components, including bodies.

In 1932, the model Nine took over from the Junior, and a sports version arrived in 1933. The following year, the Eleven was presented. This featured a side-valve engine and independent front suspension.

A new Ten model was to fill the gap between the Junior and the larger six-cylinder models, but sales were poor. After this, things started to deteriorate and two Coventry plants were closed. In 1937 the company changed its name to Singer Motors Ltd.

1936 saw the 9hp Bantam introduced and in 1939 the Nine Roadster. In 1945, the company converted its factories for war work – making parts for the Spitfire, Wellington and Halifax aircraft.

Left: The new underslung racy Singer Nine Sports Le Mans in 1933.

Standard

Standard's advertising slogan during the 1920s was 'Count them on the road'; it was a time when the Coventry-based firm was Britain's third-largest motor manufacturer.

Roman legion emblem

The overhead-valve (OHV), 11.6hp models were selling at around 200 per month in 1921 and these were joined in 1922 by an OHV 8hp model, during which time a marvellous new temporary badge

came to be adopted – the standard of the IXth Roman Legion who mysteriously disappeared en masse in Caledonia a very long time ago.

In 1924, the company used the names of British Towns, villages and landmarks for their cars – including Standard's manufacturing bases at Canley and Kenilworth – and the majority of sales were down to the new 13.9hp model.

The company was expanding and 1927 saw the new 18hp, six-cylinder model slipped into schedules, alongside a smaller 9hp, four-cylinder model.

Standard worked their way through the 1930s Depression by keeping prices keen, quality high and with modern styling.

Production now took place at Canley, where conveyor-belt assembly lines had been installed. Helping to boost sales was the fastback Flying Standard range of 1935.

Above: The 1930 'Envoy Special' saloon with Stanlite sliding roof.

Top opposite: The 1923 Standard SLO4, four-seater tourer, with disc wheels rather than the normal ten-spoke artillery wheel.

Below: The 1921 overhead-valve model designed by chairman John Budge.

Left: The 1936 Standard Mulliner 2-door landaulette.

Far left: A very rare 1947 Standard Eight woodie.

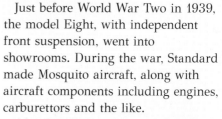

Just before World War Two in 1939, the model Eight, with independent front suspension, went into showrooms. During the war, Standard made Mosquito aircraft, along with aircraft components including engines, carburettors and the like.

After hostilities were over, Standard built tractors for Harry Ferguson. A Continental engine was used initially, but a Standard engine came later which was also used in the Vanguard World Car. A diesel followed and this too was used in the Vanguard, which was the only car made between 1948 and 1953.

Sunbeam

After World War One, the four-cylinder 16hp and 24hp six-cylinder models appeared.

In 1920 Sunbeam became part of STD Motors Ltd, which also included Talbot, Darracq and W&G Du Cros, along with equipment-makers Heenan & Froude and Jonas Woodhead.

The company, in particular the Sunbeam part of it, was heavily involved in racing, while also making road-going sports models. Old-fashioned methods were still being used, which took up time and money, and so in 1926 the competition department was closed.

In 1927, four-cylinder cars were discontinued and just three years later the straight-eight and the double-overhead-camshaft, six-

Left: The 1920 Sunbeam.

cylinder models also came to the end of their days.

In 1932, a team from Singer designed what was to become the Dawn, a mass-market vehicle for Sunbeam. It was presented in 1934 and featured a 1.6 litre overhead-valve, four-cylinder engine. Sadly, sales were poor. The STD board resigned and the company went into receivership, but Rootes rode to the rescue and salvaged Sunbeam in 1935.

At the 1937 London Motor Show, a Sunbeam was shown which was fitted with a 4½ litre overhead-valve engine. A new company was created, Sunbeam-Talbot, to produce upmarket sports models based on Rootes products including Humber and Hillman. The first two models were the Sunbeam-Talbot 10 and a 3 litre followed by a 2 litre and 4 litre model, production of which lasted until war broke out.

The 1931 Sunbeam 16hp.

Triumph

Siegfried Bettmann had arrived
in Britain from Nuremberg in
the late 19th century and, after
first selling cotton machines,
then bicycles, he finally came to
design motorcycles.

During World War One,
Triumph benefitted from all
its war work in supplying
motorcycles to the Allied forces,
but Bettmann wanted to do more
than make motor bikes. After the
war, manager Claude Holbrook
persuaded him to buy a defunct
factory in Coventry and look at
building cars.

In 1921 they bought the old
Dawson Car Company factory,
and two years later the first
Triumph car came off the
production line, a conventional,
four-cylinder vehicle designed by
Arthur Alderson of Lea Francis.

In 1924, it was joined by
a larger vehicle, the 1,873cc,

The 1,203cc Triumph Scorpion, 1931.

13/35hp, the first British car to have Lockheed hydraulic brakes on all four wheels. With an increase in engine size to 2,169cc, it was produced until 1930 – many of these models ended up in Australia. The Super Seven was presented in 1927. This was a light car using an 832cc, 21hp engine designed by Stanley Edge.

The Depression hit Triumph hard, with diminished sales for

Top: The 1934 Triumph Gloria Six.

Left: A 1934 eight-cylinder Dolomite.

both the car company and the motorcycle division.

Smaller cars were gradually phased out in the mid-1930s, with larger four- and six-cylinder models taking their place, namely Southern Cross, Gloria, Vitesse and Dolomite.

In 1935, a new factory was bought from White & Poppe, but the underlying truth was that losses were piling up. New monies were found and a fresh range of cars presented in 1937. The line-up of models was the largest ever and consisted

of four-cylinder Glorias, and four- and six-cylinder Vitesse and Dolomite models.

There were plans to buy the bankrupt Riley company in 1938, but Lord Nuffield stepped in with a better offer. In March 1939, the new low-priced Twelve was put on the market, but development costs had taken their toll and Triumph went into receivership.

Factories were sold off, which set the company up for the construction of aircraft and aero engines for the war effort.

The 1938 Triumph Dolomite Roadster.

Vauxhall

In 1925, General Motors bought Vauxhall and for the first couple of years not too much changed. The first GM-inspired vehicle was the R-type 20/60, a 2.8 litre, six-cylinder model, later uprated to become the T80 with a 3.2 litre engine.

The first real effects of the GM takeover were seen in 1931 with the introduction of the Cadet, a 2 litre, six-cylinder car with three-speed synchromesh gearbox

Above: 1931 Vauxhall Cadet VY 17hp.

Left: The 1926 OE-type 30.

– the first British car to feature this – from 1932. At the 1937 London Motor Show, Vauxhall presented their H-type Ten, which featured a four-cylinder, 1,203cc engine and was of unitary construction (the chassis and bodywork were integrated into one another), a design that was passed on to all other models before World War Two.

Right: The 1937 Vauxhall H-type.

Boom & Bust
1945 to the 1990s

In 1950, 75 per cent of British car production was exported, making the UK the largest motor vehicle exporter. This was partly due to limited competition from Europe and the demand for vehicles in the USA and Australia being greater than could be supplied by domestic production. By the mid-1950s, America had caught up and Europe too had now begun to recover from the effects of the war.

A plethora of cars was introduced directly after the war, many of which have become classics today. Aston Martin introduced their DB1 in 1948, the Morris Minor, designed by Issigonis, and the last of the RM series of Rileys, the RMC, to name but a few.

Right: The Morris Minor, 1948.

Above: The elegant Rolls-Royce Silver Cloud Series I.

Below: The Jaguar XK120. The SS name had been dropped after the war.

In the early 1950s, there was a boom in car sales; a number of other classics were introduced. First off, the beautiful Jaguar XK models of which the 120 was the first, the MG TF series, the Rolls-Royce Silver Cloud and Sunbeam Alpine... the list goes on and on!

Above: Originally seen as a stopgap while the MGA was being readied, the TF was launched in 1953 to mixed reactions.

Right: The Sunbeam Alpine was named after its success in the rally of the same name. This model was raced by a very young Stirling Moss.

After World War Two, the Bristol Aeroplane Company (BAC) needed to diversify, and so they created a car division, which became The Bristol Car Company in 1954. H. J. Aldington, director of AFN and still in the army, travelled regularly to war-torn Germany and it was at the BMW factory that he took detailed plans of their cars along with a number of development engines, which he sent back to Bristol. Unsurprisingly, Bristol based their first model on the best features of two excellent pre-war BMWs.

This included the engine from the 328 and the frame from the 326. These were complemented by a mainly steel body – although the bonnet, door and boot skins were aluminium – inspired by the BMW 327. The Bristol 400 was introduced to the market in 1947.

Based heavily on the BMW 326 frame and with a 328 engine, this is the 1947 Bristol 400. Right: The similarity to the BMW 328 is obvious.

In 1952 Austin merged with Nuffield to create the British Motor Corporation (BMC). This now included Austin, Morris, MG, Riley and Wolseley, with a 40 per cent share of the market.

The British sports car company Austin-Healey was created in 1952, a joint venture between the Austin section of BMC and the Donald Healey Motor Company. 1953 saw a specially streamlined Austin-Healey break several world land speed records at the Bonneville Salt Flats in Utah.

Their first road car was the BN1 Austin-Healey 100; in 1956, they introduced the 100/6 and, in 1959, the amazing Healey 3000, with the smaller Healey Sprite following in 1958.

Right: A beautiful example of a 1964 Austin-Healey 3000 MkIII.

Inset: The 1958 Austin-Healey 100/6.

When the Austin-Healey 3000 ceased production, Donald Healey approached Jensen Motors, famous for their V8 Interceptor range in the 1960s. Developments saw Donald become chairman of Jensen and the Jensen-Healey was designed through a joint venture with them and his son in 1972.

The AC company restarted production in 1947 with their 2 litre model, using the 1,991cc engine, and in 1953 they introduced the Ace, which featured a lightweight chassis designed by John Tojeiro. The AC Ace-Bristol came in 1957, which was raced at Le Mans in 1957 and 1958. 1954 saw the Aceca

Right: The AC Cobra had an extensive racing career under Carroll Shelby.

Below: Jensen Interceptors hand-built in West Bromwich from 1966 to 1976. The body was designed by Carrozzeria Touring and the car used a Chrysler V8 engine.

introduced and a larger four-seater, the Greyhound, also went on sale. A limited production of the Ace with a Ford Zephyr 2.6 litre engine became available in 1961, and the following year Carroll Shelby approached AC, suggesting they fit a small block V8 into the Ace – this became the AC Cobra. In the 1970s, a more powerful car was introduced, and this is today's much-sought-after classic – the AC 427 Cobra. In 1965, AC introduced their Frua-styled grand tourer aimed at wealthier customers, but only a few examples were made. After some development problems, a new car, the 3000ME, was introduced in 1979.

Alvis production started after the war with the four-cylinder TA14, followed by the 3 litre, six-cylinder TA21. Several Graber-bodied cars were displayed at the 1955 Paris Motor Show. Various models were produced during the 1960s and 1970s; Alvis became part of Rover and then British Leyland.

Five companies dominated the UK market in 1955: 90 per cent was taken up by BMC, Ford, Rootes, Standard-Triumph and Vauxhall (GM); the remainder went to smaller companies, such as Rover and Jaguar.

Above: A well-preserved TA21, although it is wearing non-standard wire wheels.

Right: Minis used a BMC A-series water-cooled, four-cylinder engine, fitted transversely.

With the Suez Crisis in 1956 and the rationing of fuel, companies looked to produce cars that were economical. The most famous was the BMC Mini. Alec Issigonis had previously designed the Morris Minor, which was still popular. In October 1957, he and his small team designed and built the original Mini prototype, affectionately known as 'The Orange Box' due to its colour.

It was different from anything on the road at the time because of its transversely positioned engine, front-wheel drive, and a suspension system with compact rubber cones instead of conventional springs. It was a huge success. Another popular BMC series was launched in 1962, the 1100 and 1300 range, again designed by Issigonis with many Mini elements.

The Rootes Group designed and built their own small car in 1963, the Hillman Imp. It was a direct competitor to the Mini and had a space-saving, rear-engine design with rear-wheel-drive layout.

The Imp was never a big success and between that, lack of investment in the Linwood plant and industrial unrest, the Rootes Group found itself with major headaches.

A partnership was negotiated by Lord William Rootes in 1964, but he died shortly afterwards and in

1967 the company
was acquired by Chrysler
Europe. There was a great deal of
badge engineering being implemented
within the Roots empire: the Singer
Chamois coupé was basically a
Hillman Imp, or vice-versa!

*Main image: The Hillman Imp was
launched in 1963. Top: The little 875cc
engine was slanted at 45 degrees to
help it fit into the rear compartment.
Bottom: The Singer Chamois coupé.*

Ford were not to be outdone and in 1959 introduced their fourth attempt, the rather unconventionally styled 105E Anglia. The car was given a new engine, a 997cc overhead-valve (OHV) straight four-cylinder unit with an over-square cylinder bore that became known as the 'Kent' engine.

The car remained in production until 1967, when it was replaced by the Escort, another remarkably popular Ford model.

Below: One of the most exciting Escort models was the Mexico, based on rally cars of the period.

Vauxhall also introduced their popular Viva range in 1963, which was their first small car since 1936. It featured a 1,057cc OHV, four-cylinder engine and only came as a two-door saloon.

1960 had seen the UK slip down the table of world car producers from second to third place, which was mainly due to an over-reliance on old-fashioned, labour-intensive methods, coupled with over-large model ranges.

Standard-Triumph, keen to reduce costs, implemented a modern volume production system, which nearly led them into bankruptcy; they were only saved when they were bought by Leyland Motors, a commercial vehicle company, in 1960. 1961 saw the presentation of the Bristol 407 which now used the larger Chrysler V8 engine. All post-1961 cars had Chrysler engines, including the Fighter and Blenheim models.

The Vauxhall Viva HA was announced in 1963. It was Vauxhall's first serious step into the compact car market after World War Two.

In 1962 Ford of Britain launched the Mk I Cortina, a family-sized car that was designed to be cheap to run and easy and inexpensive to produce in Britain. A Ford Lotus Cortina was offered in 1963, but only as a two-door saloon, all in white with a contrasting green side flash down each flank. It had a unique 1,557cc twin-cam engine

by Lotus. These cars were soon vying for top spot on the domestic market.

Competition in the family-size car also came from the BMC AD07 in 1964, better known as the Austin 1800, also badge-engineered as the Morris 1800 and Wolseley 18/85.

The classic MkI Lotus Cortina – fast and furious!

Vauxhall introduced their competitor for family car in 1957, namely the Victor.

It took much of its styling from the Chevrolet Bel Air of the same year and the production run was 390,000.

There was a bench seat at the front and the interior was clad in Rayon and 'Elastofab', with two-colour interior being standard.

The Rootes Group were determined not to be left behind. They launched their Hillman Hunter model in 1966. It used a 1,725cc engine and several versions were launched, including the GT and GLS, which had a specially tuned Holbay engine with twin-Weber carburettor.

Rover launched their modern-looking P6 in 1963. It was marketed as the Rover 2000 and was an advanced design for the time, intended to appeal to more people than their previous P4 and P5 models. First winner of the 'European Car of the Year' award, it became the most popular luxury car of the 1960s.

Opposite: The original Vauxhall Victor launched on 28 February 1957.

Above: The Rover 100 P4 was introduced in 1959.

Right: The new P6 Rover was voted European Car of the Year in 1964, the very first winner of this title.

On the sports car front, the incredible Jaguar E-type, designed by Malcolm Sayer, took the biscuit. Coupé and Roadster versions were launched in 1961; they looked amazingly fast and were able to reach 145mph.

MG produced their popular MGB and Triumph came out with the Spitfire. Before the end of the 1960s, Ford introduced their sporting Capri model, which was initially powered by a four-cylinder engine but which would later incorporate a V6 unit. It was one of the first machines to feature proper suspension and be capable of travelling at higher than normal speeds on the roads.

This is possibly the oldest surviving MGB in the UK. The first cars used the engine and gearbox from the MGA.

XDR 554

The Triumph MkI, a popular little sports car.

British Motor Holdings (BMH) was created in 1966 when Jaguar and BMC merged and, in 1967, Leyland acquired Rover, while Chrysler UK took over the Rootes Group. The following year, the government brokered the merger of Leyland-Triumph-Rover and the now struggling BMH to create British Leyland, Europe's fourth-largest car-maker. They announced a new and modern range of cars, but sadly the enterprise was plagued by internal disputes, rivalries and unattractive models such as the Austin Allegro and Morris Marina, which were slated by the motoring press.

Left: The early 1970s saw the introduction of the Series III E-type Jaguar; a massive V12 engine was fitted that could take the car to 146mph. This came at a cost. The E-type returned a meagre 14 miles to the gallon!

Top: The Austin Allegro Equipe, a specialized version of the model.

Below: The Morris Marina was manufactured by Morris from 1971 until 1980. It was sold in various markets as the Austin Marina, the Leyland Marina or the Morris 1700.

Japanese, French and German makes found a good market in the UK during the early 1970s and became very popular with their modern and attractive designs, as well as their competitive prices. Although the UK market adopted the hatchback style and front-wheel-drive format, these came several years after the European models.

For the larger-car sector, the Princess 1800/2000 was presented in 1975, marketed in its early years as either Austin, Morris or Wolseley. Chrysler also launched their Alpine in the same year, which had front-wheel drive and a hatchback. In 1976, the Rover SD1 was launched, one of the first luxury models to be given a hatchback.

Left: The Rover SD1 was the code name for this car as well as the production designation.

Below: The MGB GT, the V8 version. The badge on the grille is a give-away as was the engine tone when started up.

By now Britain had plummeted in the world car manufacturers' rankings to sixth place and, in 1975, both BLMC and Chrysler approached the government for financial help. Lord Ryder led a government inquiry into BLMC and suggested it needed substantial investment to enable it to improve productivity via mechanization, and improved labour relations. In the meantime, Chrysler received a loan. BLMC became British Leyland after nationalization in 1975, but things remained unstable and in an effort to increase productivity they reduced their workforce and plant. When the Triumph factory closed in 1980, the city of Coventry felt the blow, with thousands becoming unemployed.

The new Thatcher government of 1979 still supported BL financially and a new mass-market range was planned; this included the Mini Metro, Maestro and Montego, which were launched between 1980 and 1986. In July 1986, BL was renamed the Rover Group.

Above: The Montego was the replacement for the Morris Ital and Austin Ambassador ranges to give British Leyland an all-new competitor to the Ford Sierra and Vauxhall Cavalier. The Mini Metro (below) was a supermini, produced by British Leyland (BL) and later, the Rover Group, from 1980 to 1997.

Ford had produced its own front-wheel-drive small car, the Fiesta, but in the main had kept rear-wheel drive for its larger cars, such as the Sierra presented in 1982. The Orion saloon was launched in 1983, which used the Escort floor pan.

The Fiesta (above) was an all-new car in the supermini segment, the smallest made by Ford. This is the 1,300cc model from 1983.

The Sierra was unveiled in 1982 at the Motor Show at the NEC in Birmingham. It replaced the now ageing Cortina.

Left: It was 1981 when John Cooper introduced his own Metro Cooper, sold through his ARG dealerships.

Above: The Metro Turbo had the most powerful production A-series engine ever. It was produced from 1983 to 1990 and used the 1,275cc overhead-valve engine.

During the 1980s, foreign car-makers continued to gain ground in the British market.

In 1986, Nissan was the first Japanese car-maker to open a factory in Europe, specifically in Sunderland. They started manufacturing their mid-range Bluebird models, but it was the Micra that proved to be their best-seller during the 1980s.

The 1980s saw the disappearance of several long-established car brands. Production of MG sports cars ended in 1980, although the higher-performance Metro, Maestro and Montego continued to carry the badge. That same year, the Triumph factory in Canley closed and the Morris marque, which had been around for 70 years, was also discontinued. By 1988, the Austin marque was no longer either.

Above: The Astra name originated with Vauxhall's 1980 model, though the car was launched as the Opel Kadett D.

Right: The Carlton was upgraded by Lotus to be a 177mph sports saloon.

Left: This is the 1993 Vauxhall Cavalier. The very first Cavalier to be made at Vauxhall's Luton plant was driven off the production line by Eric Fountain, Vauxhall's manufacturing director, on 26 August 1977.

Above: In 1995, the MGF became the third all-new car to be launched by the Rover Group since the BMW takeover.

Right: The 1996 Lotus Elise weighed 1,598lb and could accelerate from 0 to 60mph in 5.8 seconds.

The Rover Group venture with Honda came to an end in 1994 when they were sold to BMW, which meant that for the first time in 112 years the UK no longer had a British-owned volume car-maker, although BMW revived the MG marque with the MGF sports car.

Meanwhile, Lotus enjoyed success with their sporty Elise model.

Peugeot commenced the production of their 309 model at Ryton in 1985 and, during the 1990s, production of the 306 and 206 also started. Toyota opened a new factory in Burnaston near Derby in 1992.

In 1987, Ford bought Aston Martin and two years later followed that up by taking over Jaguar. Production of a new small Jaguar, the X-type, commenced at the Halewood plant in 2000, and by the end of the century Ford had also bought Land Rover.

Old Names, New Owners
2000 Onwards

CHAPTER

In 2000, the Rover Group was broken up. BMW retained the Mini, while Land Rover was sold to Ford. The MG and Rover marques were acquired by the Phoenix Consortium, who changed their name to MG Rover, and began looking for possible joint ventures. By 2004, the company was heavily in debt and, although SAIC looked at buying MG Rover, talks failed and the company went into receivership in 2005. A few months later, Nanjing Automobile bought the assets and partially opened Longbridge with a small workforce in preparation for the relaunch of the MG TF in 2008. In 2016 SAIC Motors were producing the MG3 and MG6 at the Longbridge plant.

Right: The Longbridge-made MG3.

MG 3

Ford announced that car assembly at their Dagenham plant would finish in 2002, thus ending 90 years of Ford passenger car assembly in the UK.

They would, though, invest in a diesel engine facility at Dagenham, which would become their largest diesel engine centre in the world. In 2016, they announced a £181 million investment into new low-emission engines at their Bridgend plant in Wales.

After the closure of the Vauxhall assembly plant in Luton in 2003, Ellesmere Port remained the only Vauxhall assembly plant in the UK, where in 2016 the Astra model was still made.

The 2016 Vauxhall Astra.

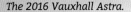

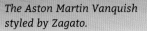

*The Aston Martin Vanquish
styled by Zagato.*

A long history of Jaguar cars ended in 2004 when due to large losses at the company, the Browns Lane plant in Coventry was closed.

Peugeot closed its Ryton plant in 2006, moving production to Slovakia and in 2007 Ford sold Aston Martin to a British-led consortium, while agreeing to supply components, including engines.

By 2016, a mix of models was being produced, including the Vantage, Vulcan and even a Lagonda Taraf.

In 2008, Ford sold Jaguar Land Rover to Tata Motors of India, who in 2015 announced more than £1 billion of investment and 1,300 new UK jobs.

In 2016, Jaguar introduced their brand-new I-Pace concept, alongside the F-Pace, F-type, XE, XJ and XF models. Meanwhile Range Rover were making the Range Rover Sport and Evoque models.

The brand-new Jaguar I-Pace concept. This car sees Jaguar looking to an electronic future.

Above: The Range Rover Evoque hit five years of UK production in 2016.
Below: The 2016 Jaguar F-Pace SUV.

The year 2011 saw BMW announce the extension of the Mini range. Countryman, Clubman and Convertible were just three models for 2016.

On the sports car scene, McLaren Automotive produced a startling array of models for 2016, from the 570S through to the incredible P1 GTR. Lotus Cars also had a great range of sporting models, from the Exige range through to the Evora and Elise models.

Below: BMW's 2016 Mini Countryman.

Top: The McLaren 570 GT with panoramic roof.   Below: The 2016 Lotus Exige Sport 380.

TVR, a company that dates to 1947 – having already produced several exciting sports cars, Griffith, Tuscan, Vixen, Taimar and Tasmin, to name but a few – announced their new car project in 2015, which features innovative design and styling, and includes F1-inspired ground-effect technology. Power comes via a Cosworth-tuned and -enhanced V8 engine. Their Welsh factory immediately found itself busy fulfilling orders that ran through to the end of 2018.

Top: In line with TVR's traditional DNA, this is the 2018 Griffith, which looks great, sounds great and has great performance.

Above: The Bentley Bentayga.

Opposite top: The 2016 Ghost model from Rolls-Royce.

Right: The Bentley Mulsanne Speed – named after the famous straight at the Le Mans race circuit.

These days, Bentley have a great model range with some very familiar names: Mulsanne, Flying Spur, Continental and Bentayga, while Rolls-Royce also have a selection of models with equally familiar names: Phantom, Ghost, Wraith and Dawn.

Bright future

In 2016, the SMMT posted that there are more than 30 manufacturers building more than 70 separate models of vehicles in the UK. The industry is supported by more than 2,000 component providers and some of the world's most skilled engineers. The motor industry is innovating fast, with vehicles now being 42 per cent more fuel-efficient than they were in 2000 and the UK is seen internationally as a leading centre of automotive R&D.

To maintain its excellent position, the UK must grasp the opportunities of breakthrough technologies – connected and autonomous vehicles – and secure the benefits for the UK economy and society. According to analysts, connected and autonomous vehicles could potentially create an additional 320,000 jobs in the UK by 2030, 25,000 of which would be in automotive manufacturing.

At the start of 2019, the UK government was looking to secure a deal with the EU that would safeguard Britain's crucial automotive industry.

The Rolls-Royce Dawn, which was named the Daily Telegraph's *'Luxury Car of the Year', 2016.*

Picture Credits

The Author and Publisher would like to thank the following people and organizations
for their kind help and contribution:

Mr P de Rousset-Hall & ACOC Archive	106, 108/109
Auto Carriers Ltd & ACOC Archive	41
Mr J Crabb & ACOC Archive	40/41
AC (Acedes) Cars Ltd & ACOC Archive	108t
Sir Henry Royce Memorial Foundation	82/83
Auckland War Memorial Museum, Auckland, New Zealand	24/25
Daimler AG	8, 9,10, 11, 12t, 13, 15b, 16/17
Humber Register	58t, 59, 60, 60/61, 128/129
Lagonda Club	62/63, 64/65
Lakeland Motor Museum	25, 26t
Louwman museum, the Netherlands	22/23
National Motor Museum, Beaulieu. UK	18/19, 20/21, 32/33, 33, 55, 56, 56/57, 70, 70/71, 74, 156/157, 158/159, 166/167, 168/169, 171t, 172/173,176/177
Swift Owners Club	14/15, 34, 35b.
Talbot Owners Club	46/47, 48/49, 120/121, 122/123
The Rootes Archive Centre Trust	54, 126, 164/165
US Library of Congress	38/39, 104/105
Vintage Austin Register UK	44/45
Wolseley Owners Club	30, 31
Wolverhampton Archives, Wolverhampton, West Midlands	26b, 27, 94/95, 96/97, 98/99

All Standard images were kindly supplied by David Groom – Archivist
of the Standard Register and the Edwardian and Vintage 1903–1930.
Archivist of the Standard Motor Club.   88, 89, 90/91, 92/93, 160t, 160 inset, 161, 162/163

Aston Martin
Bentley Motors Ltd
BMW
Ford UK
Jaguar, Land Rover
Lotus Cars
McLaren Automotive
MG
Rolls-Royce
Rover
TVR
Vauxhall Motors

All other images come from the Author's collection.